Mel Bay presents

400 YEARS OF RECORDER MUSIC

by Dr. William M. Weiss

Recorder Anthology
Four Hundred Years

Musical Anthologies and Collections reflect the tastes and interests of the collector who for personal reasons selects the pieces that are appealing for their melodic, rhythmic, harmonic, form and historical significance.

This Anthology represents a small sampling from the vast reservoir of music composed and published during the 400 years extending from the early Renaissance through the Baroque, Rocco, Classic and early Romantic Periods.

The music of historically well-known as well as lesser-known and obscure composers has been included in the Anthology. Solos, duets, some trios and quartets from the various periods and schools, German, Italian, French and English, have been chosen because of their musical content and charm, primarily, and because they illustrate and typify the musical values of the eras in which they were composed. In some instances, keys have been transposed, signatures and bar lines have been added especially in Bicinium duets of the Renaissance Period.

Separate movements, taken from sonatas and suites, have been included as well as some thematic material. Vocal pieces have been transcribed for the recorder following a tradition established in the early renaissance period when instruments and voices were freely interchangeable.

This practice has been extended, by the author, into the 18th and 19th centuries.

The Anthology has been, primarily, arranged for the descant or soprano recorder. The alto, tenor and bass recorders, however, are included and coded where indicated, in duets, trios and quartets.*

Phrasing and breath marks have been indicated as well as tempo and dynamic signs in most instances. They are to be observed at the discretion of the players. Not all the pieces are marked since individual performers may decide on their own tempo and dynamic ranges.

There are no clear-cut lines of demarcation separating the various eras and periods, but generally acknowledged time frames with much overlapping are accepted. The periods are as follows:

Renaissance 1450 - 1600
Baroque 1600 - 1750
Rocco 1725 - 1775
Classic 1775 - 1825
Early Romantic 1820 - 1850

*Code

S — Soprano Recorder
A — Alto Recorder
T — Tenor Recorder
B — Bass Recorder

Composers — Recorder Anthology*
15th - 16th - 17th - 18th - 19th Centuries

✳ Bicinium

Jean de Okeghem
(Ca. 1430 – 1495)

✳ Bicinium

Anonymous
(1400 – 1500)

* A two-part song. It is an archaic term-name formerly used in Germany for any short-two part composition.

4

*Vocal Catch

Antoine Brumel
(1460 – Ca 1520)

Vocal Catch

Antoine Brumel

* Catch-English Round. Songs are commentary on society with satire and puns intended.

Bicinium

Josquin des Prés
(1445 – 1521)

6

Teremu Tu

French Chanson

Jacotin (D.1529)

7

Gavotte

Henry la Jeune
(1523 — 1600)

Dance

Hans Gerle
(1532 — 1570)

Two Dances

Pierre Phalesius
(1510 — 1573)

a) Allemande

b) Bransle

10

Bicinium

Orlando di Lasso
(1532 – 1594)

Bicinium

Orlando di Lasso

Galiardo

William Byrd
(1542 – 1623)

13

"Was Will Ich Mehr Von Ihr"
(What More Could I Ask of Her)

Leonhart Lechner
(1550 – 1606)

La Volta

Thomas Morley
(1557 – 1603)

Bicinium

Adam Gumpelzhaimer
(1559 – 1625)

A Catch I

Adam Gumpelzhaimer

A Catch II

16

"Welcome Sweet Pleasure"

Thomas Weelkes
(1575 – 1623)

Melody

Anon (1600)

Thema Volkslied

Anon (1600)

Bicinium

Anon (1500-1600)

18

Rounds I

Dr. John Blow
(1649 – 1708)

II

III

* Second player starts when first player reaches this point. Like wise third player starts when second player reaches this point.

3 Voices – Vocal Catch "On the Battle at Hailbron"

Dr. John Blow

* start 𝄋

* Second then third voice start when first voice reaches this point.

Menuet

George Muffat
(1645 – 1704)

Gavotte

George Muffat

Sarabande

Arcangelo Corelli
(1653 — 1713)

Theme — Sonata

Archangelo Corelli

21

A Catch I

Henry Purcell
(1658 – 1695)

A Catch II

Henry Purcell

A Catch III

Henry Purcell

Menuet

Henry Purcell

Arioso

Alessandro Scarlatti
(1659 – 1725)

23

Little Dance

Johann C. F. Fischer
(1660 − d. circa 1738)

24

Slow Dance

Johann C. F. Fischer

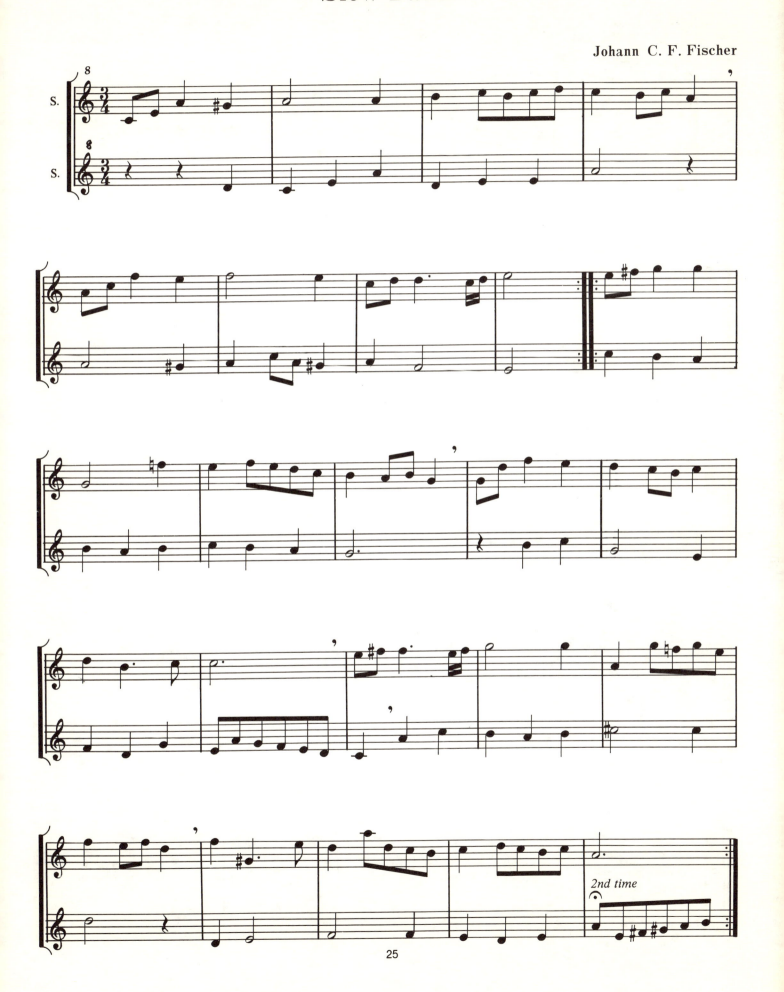

25

"Les Chérubins ou l'aimable Lazure"

Francois Couperin
(1668 – 1733)

26

Dance

Francois Couperin

Sonata
Two Movements

Antonio Vivaldi
(Ca 1676 – 1741)

Theme‑Sonata

Jean Loeillet
(1680 − 1730)

Sonata I

Johann C. Schickhardt
(1680 – 1740)

29

Sonata II

Johann C. Schickhardt

Largo

Georg P. Telemann
(1681 – 1767)

Minuet

Georg P. Telemann

31

Gigue

Georg P. Telemann

Allegretto

Rigaudon

Jean P. Rameau
(1683 – 1764)

Allegretto

32

Rigaudon

Jean P. Rameau

We Gather Here, Good Neighbors All
from "Peasants' Cantata"

Johann S. Bach
(1685 – 1750)

Polonaise
from "Anna Magdalena Bach Book"

Johann S. Bach

Menuet

Johann S. Bach

Menuet
from "Anna Magdalena Bach Note Book"

Johann S. Bach

35

Musette
from "Anna Magdalena Bach Book"

Johann S. Bach

Menuet

Johann S. Bach

Moderato

Sonata–Movement

George F. Handel

Tempo di Gavotli

37

Minuet

George F. Handel
(1685 – 1759)

Sonata – Movement *

George F. Handel

✳ *This movement leads directly into the next with a slight pause.*

Sonata — Movement

George F. Handel

Impertinence
from "Aylesford Pieces"

George F. Handel

Minuet

Leonarda Vinci
(1690 – 1730)

41

Musette I – Baroque

Anon
(1700 – 1800)

Fine

Musette II

Anon

*Repeat Musette I

Lamentarola

Anon
18 Century

Siciliano

Anon
18th Century

43

March

Nicholas Chedeville
(1705 – 1782)

Rigaudon

Nicholas Chedeville

Gavotte

Giovanni Martini
(1706 – 1784)

Air

Samuel Howard
(1710 – 1782)

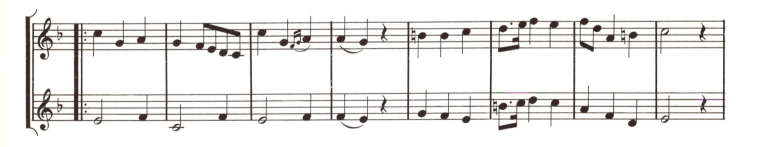

Air

Dr. Thomas Arne
(1710 – 1778)

46

Air

Dr. Thomas Arne

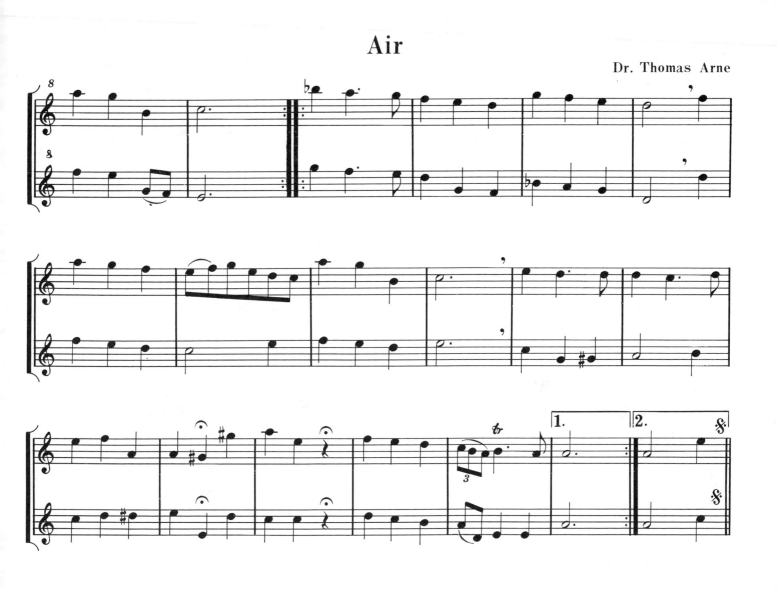

"The Lass With the Delicate Air"

Dr. Thomas Arne

Dance

Christoph W. Gluck
(1714 – 1787)

Minuet I

Leopold Mozart
(1719 – 1787)

48

Minuet II

Leopold Mozart

Melody

D.C. al Fine "Minuet I"

"Pied Piper"

Nicola Piccini
(1728 – 1800)

Allegretto

Come, Gentle Spring

from "The Seasons"

Franz J. Haydn
(1732 – 1809)

Serenade

Franz J. Haydn

Theme from "Surprise Symphony"

Franz J. Haydn

Gavotte

François J. Gossec
(1734 – 1829)

52

A Stately Dance

James Hook
(1746 – 1827)

She Flies Away
from "Don Giovanni"

Wolfgang A. Mozart
(1756 – 1791)

Voi Che Sapete
from "The Marriage of Figaro"

Wolfgang A. Mozart

Glockenspiel
from "Magic Flute"

Wolfgang A. Mozart

"Für Elise"

Ludwig V. Beethoven
(1770 – 1827)

Minuet in G

Ludwig V. Beethoven

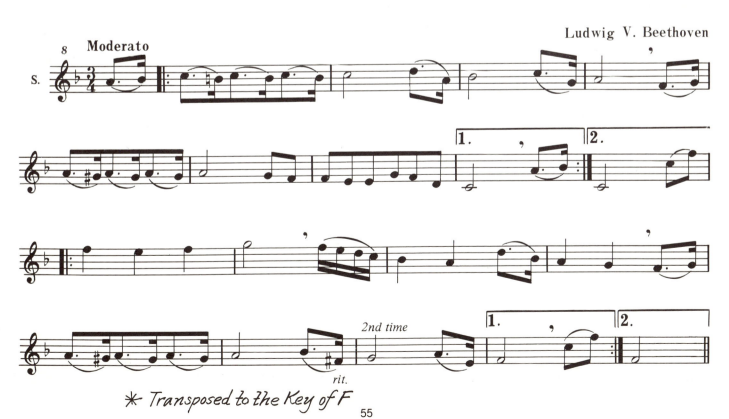

2nd time

rit.

✳ *Transposed to the Key of F*

55

Andante

Antonio Diabelli
(1781 – 1858)

56

Hunting Chorus
from "Der Freischütz"

Carl M. von Weber
(1786 – 1826)

Moment Musicale

Franz Schubert
(1797 – 1828)

58

Themes from Overture – "Rosamunde"

Franz Schubert

Theme – "Rosamunde"

Franz Schubert

The Brooklet

Franz Schubert

The Trout

Franz Schubert

It Is Better to Laugh Than Be Sighing
from "Lucrezia Borgia"

Gaetano Donizetti
(1797 – 1848)

Mazurka

Frédéric Chopin
(1810 – 1849)

The Wild Horseman

Robert Schumann
(1810 – 1856)

Fine

D.C. al Fine

"In the Forest"

Felix Mendelssohn
(1809 – 1847)

Theme from "Les Preludes"

Franz Liszt
(1811 – 1886)

Drinking Song
from – "La Traviata"

Giuseppe Verdi
(1813 – 1901)